Dachshunds

by Grace Hansen

Abdo Kids Jumbo is an Imprint of Abdo Kids
abdobooks.com

abdobooks.com

Published by Abdo Kids, a division of ABDO, P.O. Box 398166, Minneapolis, Minnesota 55439.
Copyright © 2022 by Abdo Consulting Group, Inc. International copyrights reserved in all countries.
No part of this book may be reproduced in any form without written permission from the publisher.
Abdo Kids Jumbo™ is a trademark and logo of Abdo Kids.

Printed in China

052021

092021

THIS BOOK CONTAINS
RECYCLED MATERIALS

Photo Credits: Alamy, iStock, Minden Pictures, Shutterstock, Thinkstock

Production Contributors: Teddy Borth, Jennie Forsberg, Grace Hansen
Design Contributors: Dorothy Toth, Pakou Moua

Library of Congress Control Number: 2020947651
Publisher's Cataloging-in-Publication Data

Names: Hansen, Grace, author.

Title: Dachshunds / by Grace Hansen

Description: Minneapolis, Minnesota : Abdo Kids, 2022 | Series: Dogs | Includes online resources and
    index.

Identifiers: ISBN 9781098206017 (lib. bdg.) | ISBN 9781098206574 (ebook) | ISBN 9781098206857
    (Read-to-Me ebook)

Subjects: LCSH: Dachshunds--Juvenile literature. | Hunting dogs--Juvenile literature. | Dogs--Juvenile
    literature. | Animal behavior--Juvenile literature.

Classification: DDC 599.772--dc23

Table of Contents

Dachshunds

Dachshunds are as cute as they are long! But they were not **bred** to be cute.

Pronounced dahks-hund, the dog's name is made up of two German words. *Dachs* is German for badger. *Hund* means dog.

These dogs were **bred** more than 600 years ago. Their main job was to hunt badgers. Badgers are **tough** animals. But the small, **sturdy** dachshund is tougher!

badger

Dachshunds have low, long bodies. They are the perfect size and shape to get into badger dens.

Dachshunds come in two sizes. Standard dachshunds are 8 to 9 inches (20 to 23 cm) tall. Minis are 5 to 6 inches (13 to 15 cm) tall.

Dachshunds have three coat types. Smooth coats are short and soft. They are easy to groom and keep clean.

wire
smooth

Longhaired dachshunds were **bred** for places with cooler weather. Dogs with **wire** coats can hunt in places with **dense** or thorny surroundings. The wiry hair protects the skin.

Dachshunds' coats can be many colors, like red, black, cream, and tan. They can also have different markings.

Personality

Dachshunds were **bred** to be **independent** hunters. However, they are still social and want to be with their families. Their bold personalities and sweet faces make them easy to love.

More Facts

- Dachshunds tend to live longer than many dog breeds. Most live 12 to 15 years.

- A dachshund named Chanel once held the title of oldest-living dog. She lived to be 21 years old!

- Dachshunds are members of the American Kennel Club (AKC) Hound Group. They are the group's smallest members!

Glossary

bred – developed over time for a certain purpose.

dense – thick and hard to see through or move through.

independent – not needing the support of another.

sturdy – strong, hardy, or solid.

wire – firm and stiff.

Index

Abdo Kids ONLINE
FREE! ONLINE MULTIMEDIA RESOURCES

Visit **abdokids.com** to access crafts, games, videos, and more!